Mug Cakes

Dessert Lovers

Easy Mug Cake Recipes That Will Impress Everyone

BY: Allie Allen

COOK & ENJOY

Copyright 2019 Allie Allen

Copyright Notes

This book is written as an informational tool. While the author has taken every precaution to ensure the accuracy of the information provided therein, the reader is warned that they assume all risk when following the content. The author will not be held responsible for any damages that may occur as a result of the readers' actions.

The author does not give permission to reproduce this book in any form, including but not limited to: print, social media posts, electronic copies or photocopies, unless permission is expressly given in writing.

Contents

Delicious Mug Cake Recipes

ssssssssssssssssssssssssssssssssssssssssssssssssssss

1) Strawberry Mug Cakes

These cakes are best made with fresh strawberries and are excellent if you have a sweet tooth.

Cooking Time: 4 minutes

Makes: 1

List of Ingredients:

- Flour (1 ¾ tablespoons)
- Granulated sugar (1 tablespoon)
- Baking soda (1/8 teaspoon)
- Salt (to taste)
- Strawberries (2 tablespoons, mashed)
- Canola Oil (½ teaspoons)
- White Distilled Vinegar (1/8 teaspoons)
- Vanilla extract (1/8 teaspoon)

sssssssssssssssssssssssssssssssssssssssssssssssssssssssssss

Procedure:

Mix all ingredients in a microwavable mug and place to cook on high for a minute. Cool, serve and enjoy!

2) Cherry Almond Cake in a Mug

Now you can have your kid's favorite cake right from the microwave in minutes.

Makes: 1

Cooking Time: 2 minutes

List of Ingredients:

- Almond Butter (1 tablespoon, melted)
- G. Sugar (1 tablespoon)
- Caster Sugar (1 tablespoon)
- Vanilla (1 teaspoon)
- Salt (to taste)
- Egg (1, yolk)
- Flour (2 tablespoons)
- Cherry Cake Mix (2 tablespoons)
- Cherries (¼ can)
- Whip Cream (optional topping)

ssssssssssssssssssssssssssssssssssssssssssssssssssssssss

Procedure:

Whisk all ingredients in a microwavable mug and place to cook on high for a minute. Cool and top with whipping cream and more cherries. Serve and Enjoy!

3) Cinnamon Roll Mug Cake

A hint of cinnamon can go a far way. Imagine taking it another mile in the sky by adding cream cheese ... simply delicious!

Makes: 1

Cooking Time: 5 minutes

List of Ingredients:

- Applesauce (2 tablespoons)
- Vegetable oil (1 tablespoon)
- Buttermilk (1 tablespoon)
- Vanilla (¼ teaspoon)
- Flour (¼ cup)
- Sugar (2 tablespoons)
- Cinnamon (¾ teaspoon)
- Nutmeg (¼ teaspoon)
- Baking Powder (1/8 teaspoon)
- Salt (1/8 teaspoon)
- Cream Cheese frosting (to be used as topping)

SSSSSSSSSSSSSSSSSSSSSSSSSSSSSSSSSSSSSSSSSSSSSSSSSSSSSSS

Procedure:

Whisk all ingredients (except for the cream cheese icing) in a microwavable mug and place to cook on high for a minute. Cool and top with cream cheese frosting. Serve and Enjoy!

4) Chocolate Cake Cups

These delicious cups are perfect for a night of romance or even just hanging with your young one.

Cooking Time: 3 minutes

Makes: 2

List of Ingredients:

- Flour (¼ cup)
- Sugar (¼ cup)
- Cocoa powder (¼ cup)
- Salt (pinch)
- Milk (¼ cup)
- Butter (melted, ¼ cup)
- Lightly Beaten Eggs (2, large)
- Vanilla (1 teaspoon)
- Chocolate chips (a little more than ¼ cup)

sssssssssssssssssssssssssssssssssssssssssssssssssssssss

Procedure:

Using a small bowl, mix together your dry ingredients (except the chocolate chips). Add your liquids and eggs then stir well until fully incorporated. Add chocolate chips and fold. Pour batter into two microwavable mugs and top with more chocolate chips. Place in microwave and cook on high for about 2 minutes. Cool, serve and enjoy!

5) French Vanilla Cake in a Mug

Can't bother to stand in front of the oven? Well now you don't have to! Enjoy the delicious tastes from a mug!

Makes: 1

Cooking Time: 2 minutes

List of Ingredients:

- Butter (1 tablespoon, melted)
- G. Sugar (1 tablespoon)
- Caster Sugar (1 tablespoon)
- Vanilla (1 teaspoon)
- Salt (to taste)
- Egg (1, yolk)
- Flour (2 tablespoons)
- French Vanilla Cake Mix (2 tablespoons)
- Icing Sugar (optional topping)

sssssssssssssssssssssssssssssssssssssssssssssssssssss

Procedure:

Whisk all ingredients in a microwavable mug and place to cook on high for a minute. Cool and top with icing sugar. Serve and Enjoy!

6) Chocolate Chip Cookie in a Mug

Delicious cookies in under 10 minutes that your whole family will love.

Cooking Time: 2 minutes

Makes: 1 large

List of Ingredients:

- Butter (1 tablespoon, unsalted)
- Sugar (1 tablespoon)
- Vanilla (½ teaspoons)
- Salt (1/8 tsp)
- Egg Yolk (1)
- Flour (3 tablespoons)
- Chocolate Chips (2 tablespoons)

ssssssssssssssssssssssssssssssssssssssssssssssssssssss

Procedure:

Add your butter to your mug and microwave until fully melted (just about 30 seconds). To the mug add your sugar, vanilla, salt and egg yolk. Stir until you can see no traces of the egg. Proceed to add your flour then pour in your chocolate chips. Put the mug in the microwave and allow to cook for about 45 seconds. Serve and enjoy!

7) Yellow Cake in a Mug

Why bake a whole cake when you just need a slice of heaven? This recipe will give you just that!

Makes: 1

Cooking Time: 2 minutes

List of Ingredients:

- Butter (1 tablespoon, melted)
- G. Sugar (1 tablespoon)
- Caster Sugar (1 tablespoon)
- Vanilla (1 teaspoon)
- Salt (to taste)
- Egg (1, yolk)
- Flour (2 tablespoons)
- Yellow Cake Mix (2 tablespoons)
- Icing Sugar (optional topping)

sssssssssssssssssssssssssssssssssssssssssssssssssssssss

Procedure:

Whisk all ingredients in a microwavable mug and place to cook on high for a minute. Cool and top with icing sugar. Serve and Enjoy!

8) Brownie in a Mug

Brownies are known to be from a hot oven but can you expect the same from a microwave? Of course you can, maybe, even better.

Cooking Time: 1 minute

Makes: 1

List of Ingredients:

- Butter (2 tablespoons)
- Sugar (3 tablespoons)
- Vanilla (¼ tsp)
- Salt (to taste)
- Egg (1, yolk)
- Flour (4 tablespoons)
- Cocoa powder (1 tablespoon)
- Chocolate chunks (2 tablespoons)

sssssssssssssssssssssssssssssssssssssssssssssssssssssssss

Procedure:

Allow butter to melt in the microwave in your mug. Add your sugar, salt and vanilla followed by the egg yolk. To this, add cocoa powder and flour and fold until well combined. Add your chocolate chunks the microwave on high for 45 seconds. Serve and enjoy!

9) Orange Scented Mug Cakes

This recipe for orange mug cakes creates the most amazing cake I have ever tasted. Then again, I'm a sucker for oranges.

Cooking Time: 3 minutes

Makes: 1 cupcake

List of Ingredients:

- All purpose flour (1 ½ tablespoons)
- Baking powder (¼ teaspoon)
- Baking soda (1/8 teaspoon)
- Salt (to taste)
- Extra virgin olive oil (1/3 tablespoons)
- Soy milk (1 tablespoon)
- Granulated sugar (¾ tablespoons)
- Lemon juice (¼ tablespoons)
- Orange zest (chopped finely)

sssssssssssssssssssssssssssssssssssssssssssssssssssssss

Procedure:

Whisk all ingredients in a microwavable mug and place to cook on high for a minute. Cool, serve and enjoy!

Optional: Sprinkle with a dash of Cinnamon powder before serving.

10) Chocolate Peanut Butter Mug Cake

If you love comfort food you will adore this mug cake. There's nothing better than chocolate and peanut butter.

Cooking Time: 5 minutes

Makes: 1

List of Ingredients:

- Cocoa Powder (1 tablespoon and 2 teaspoons)
- Peanut Butter (3 tablespoons, powdered)
- Salt (1/16 teaspoons)
- Sugar (1 tablespoon and 1 teaspoon)
- Baking powder (1 teaspoon)
- Coconut Oil (2 teaspoons)
- Milk (3 tablespoons)
- Vanilla (¼ teaspoons)

sssssssssssssssssssssssssssssssssssssssssssssssssssssss

Procedure:

Mix all your dry ingredients well in a mug then add in your liquids and stir well. Microwave on high for 1 min and 25 sec. Serve and Enjoy,

11) Raspberry Mug Cake

If you love raspberries you will love this recipe even more!

Cooking Time: 3 minutes

Makes: 1

List of Ingredients:

- Silken tofu (¼ tablespoons, pureed)
- Dairy free soy margarine (¾ tbsps., softened)
- Granulated sugar (1 ½ tablespoons)
- Soy yogurt-vanilla (¼ tablespoons)
- Vanilla (1/8 teaspoon)
- All purpose flour (2 tbsps.)
- Baking powder (1/8 teaspoon)
- Salt (to taste)
- Almond milk (1 tablespoon)
- Raspberries-fresh (1 tablespoon, crushed)

sssssssssssssssssssssssssssssssssssssssssssssssssssssss

Procedure:

Whisk all ingredients in a microwavable mug and place to cook on high for a minute. Cool, serve and enjoy!

12) Mug Cheesecake

Delicious cheesecake in under 5 minutes.

Cooking Time: 5 minutes

Makes: 1

List of Ingredients:

- Cream cheese (2 oz.)
- Sour cream (2 tablespoons)
- Egg (1, medium)
- Lemon juice (½ tsp)
- Vanilla (¼ tsp)
- Sugar (2 tablespoons)

sssssssssssssssssssssssssssssssssssssssssssssssssssssssss

Procedure:

Add all your ingredients into a microwavable mug. Allow to cook on high for 90 seconds (You will need to stop and stir every 30 seconds and check for doneness). Allow to cool and serve. Enjoy!

Optional: Consider topping with whipped cream and nuts.

13) Raisin and Oats Mug Cakes

Do you love oatmeal and want another way to make a creative dish with them? Why not make a mug cake?

Cooking Time: 3 minutes

Makes: 1

List of Ingredients:

- Flour (1 ½ tablespoons)
- Almond milk (1 ½ tablespoons)
- Raisins
- Baking powder (¼ teaspoon)
- Salt (to taste)
- Granulated sugar (1 ¼ tablespoons)
- Canola oil (½ tablespoons)
- Baking soda (1/8 teaspoons)
- Vanilla extract (1/8 teaspoon)
- Hazelnut extract (1/8 teaspoon)
- Oats (¾ tbsps., apple cinnamon)
- Lemon Juice (1 teaspoon)

sssssssssssssssssssssssssssssssssssssssssssssssssssss

Procedure:

Whisk all ingredients in a microwavable mug and place to cook on high for a minute. Cool, serve and enjoy!

14) Peanut Butter Cookie

Who doesn't love rich peanut butter cookies? What's even greater is now you can have it in minutes from a mug.

Makes: 1

Cooking Time: 1 minute

List of Ingredients:

- Butter (1 tablespoon)
- Peanut Butter (1 tablespoon)
- Sugar (2 tablespoons)
- Vanilla (½ teaspoons)
- Salt (to taste)
- Egg (1, yolk)
- Flour (3 tablespoons)
- Nuts (crushed, to be used as topping)

sssssssssssssssssssssssssssssssssssssssssssssssssssssssss

Procedure:

Allow butter and peanut butter to melt in the microwave in your mug. Add your sugar, salt and vanilla followed by the egg yolk. To this, add flour and fold until well combined. Microwave on high for about 35 seconds. Top with nuts, serve and enjoy!

15) Blueberry Mug cakes

These will make a delicious addition to your breakfast or for a healthy alternative to traditional sugar filled cupcakes.

Cooking Time: 3 minutes

Makes: 1

List of Ingredients:

- Silken tofu (¼ tablespoons, pureed)
- Dairy free soy margarine (¾ tbsps., softened)
- Granulated sugar (1 ½ tablespoons)
- Soy yogurt-vanilla (¼ tablespoons)
- Vanilla (1/8 teaspoon)
- All purpose flour (2 tbsps.)
- Baking powder (1/8 teaspoon)
- Salt (to taste)
- Coconut milk (1 tablespoon)
- Blueberries-fresh (1 tablespoon, crushed)

sssssssssssssssssssssssssssssssssssssssssssssssssssssssss

Procedure:

Whisk all ingredients in a microwavable mug and place to cook on high for a minute. Cool, serve and enjoy!

16) Eggless Chocolate Cake

Allergic to eggs? No problem, is an option for a sweet treat you can enjoy.

Makes: 1

Cooking Time: 2 minutes

List of Ingredients:

- Flour (2 tablespoons)
- Cocoa Powder (2 teaspoons, unsweetened)
- Baking Powder (¼ teaspoon)
- Salt (to taste)
- Milk (2 tablespoons)
- Oil (1 tablespoon)
- Chocolate chips (mini, about a handful)
- Almond Butter (1 tablespoon)

sssssssssssssssssssssssssssssssssssssssssssssssssssssss

Procedure:

Add all your ingredients into a microwavable mug. Allow to cook on high for about a minute (check for doneness every 5 seconds after the 45 second mark). Allow to cool, serve and enjoy!

Optional: Consider topping with whip cream and strawberries.

17) Easy Banana Bread

This is a healthy banana bread that you could add nuts to or eat as is.

Cooking Time: 4 minutes

Makes: 1 cake

List of Ingredients:

- Egg Replacer (½ teaspoon)
- Hot water (1/8 tablespoons)
- Flour (1 ½ tablespoons)
- Granulated sugar (¼ tablespoons)
- Baking powder (¼ teaspoon)
- Baking soda (1/8 teaspoon)
- Salt (to taste)
- Bananas (½ cup, mashed)
- Dairy-free soy margarine (½ tablespoons, melted)
- Dairy-free soy yogurt (½ teaspoons)
- Vanilla extract (1/8 teaspoon)

sssssssssssssssssssssssssssssssssssssssssssssssssssssss

Procedure:

Mix all ingredients in a microwavable mug and place to cook on high for a minute. Cool, serve and enjoy!

18) Red Velvet Cake in a Mug

You said it, enjoy your favorite delight in a matter of minutes right from the microwave.

Makes: 1

Cooking Time: 2 minutes

List of Ingredients:

- Butter (1 tablespoon, melted)
- G. Sugar (1 tablespoon)
- Caster Sugar (1 tablespoon)
- Vanilla (1 teaspoon)
- Salt (to taste)
- Egg (1, yolk)
- Flour (2 tablespoons)
- Red Velvet Cake Mix (2 tablespoons)
- Icing Sugar (optional topping)

ssssssssssssssssssssssssssssssssssssssssssssssssssssss

Procedure:

Whisk all ingredients in a microwavable mug and place to cook on high for a minute. Cool and top with icing sugar. Serve and Enjoy!

19) Lemon Scented Mug Cakes

This recipe for vegan mug cakes creates the most amazing lemon scented cakes.

Cooking Time: 3 minutes

Makes: 1 cupcake

List of Ingredients:

- All purpose flour (1 ½ tablespoons)
- Baking powder (¼ teaspoon)
- Baking soda (1/8 teaspoon)
- Salt (to taste)
- Extra virgin olive oil (1/3 tablespoons)
- Soy milk (1 tablespoon)
- Granulated sugar (¾ tablespoons)
- Lemon juice (¼ tablespoons)
- Lemon zest (chopped finely)

ssssssssssssssssssssssssssssssssssssssssssssssssssss

Procedure:

Whisk all ingredients in a microwavable mug and place to cook on high for a minute. Cool, serve and enjoy!

20) Biscoff Minute Mug Cake

So easy yet so delicious!

Makes: 1

Cooking Time: 2 minutes

List of Ingredients:

- Egg (1, beaten)
- Sugar (1 tablespoon)
- B powder (½ teaspoons)
- Flour (1 tablespoon)
- Biscoff (2 tablespoons)
- Vanilla (1 teaspoon)

sssssssssssssssssssssssssssssssssssssssssssssssssssss

Procedure:

Whisk all ingredients in a microwavable mug and place to cook on high for a minute. Cool, serve and enjoy!

21) Moist Pumpkin Mug Cake

Delicious pumpkin cake from a mug. Healthy yet breath taking, who knew it was possible?

Cooking Time: 2 minutes

Makes: 1 mug cake

List of Ingredients:

- Almond milk (1 tablespoon)
- Cider vinegar (1/8 teaspoon)
- All purpose flour (1 ¼ tablespoons)
- Baking powder (¼ teaspoon)
- Baking soda (1/8 teaspoon)
- Granulated sugar (1 teaspoon)
- Brown sugar (1 teaspoon)
- Cashews (1 tsp, ground finely)
- Cinnamon (1/8 teaspoon)
- Ginger (1/8 teaspoon)
- Nutmeg (1/8 teaspoon)
- Salt (to taste)
- Pumpkin (½ tablespoons, pureed)

- Canola oil (1/3 teaspoons)
- Sour cream (½ teaspoon, dairy free)
- Vanilla extract (1/8 teaspoon)

sssssssssssssssssssssssssssssssssssssssssssssssss

Procedure:

Whisk all ingredients in a microwavable mug and place to cook on high for a minute. Cool, serve and enjoy!

22) Oatmeal Crunch Cookies

Get delicious cookies in under 5 minutes with just a few mugs and a microwave.

Makes: 1

Cooking Time: 2 minutes

List of Ingredients:

- Butter (1 tablespoon, melted)
- G Sugar (1 tablespoon)
- B Sugar (1 tablespoon)
- Vanilla (¼ tablespoons)
- Egg (1, yolk)
- Salt (to taste)
- Flour (3 tablespoons)
- Oatmeal (1 ½ teaspoons)
- Corn Flakes (1 ½ tablespoons)

sssssssssssssssssssssssssssssssssssssssssssssssssssssss

Procedure:

Whisk all ingredients in a microwavable mug and place to cook on high for a minute. Cool, serve and enjoy!

About the Author

Allie Allen developed her passion for the culinary arts at the tender age of five when she would help her mother cook for their large family of 8. Even back then, her family knew this would be more than a hobby for the young Allie and when she graduated from high school, she applied to cooking school in London. It had always been a dream of the young chef to study with some of Europe's best and she made it happen by attending the Chef Academy of London.

After graduation, Allie decided to bring her skills back to North America and open up her own restaurant. After 10 successful years as head chef and owner, she decided to sell her business and pursue other career avenues. This monumental decision led Allie to her true calling, teaching. She also started to write e-books for her students to study at home for practice. She is now the proud author of several e-books and gives private and semi-private cooking lessons to a range of students at all levels of experience.

Stay tuned for more from this dynamic chef and teacher when she releases more informative e-books on cooking and baking in the near future. Her work is infused with stores and anecdotes you will love!

Author's Afterthoughts

I can't tell you how grateful I am that you decided to read my book. My most heartfelt thanks that you took time out of your life to choose my work and I hope you find benefit within these pages.

There are so many books available today that offer similar content so that makes it even more humbling that you decided to buying mine.

Tell me what you thought! I am eager to hear your opinion and ideas on what you read as are others who are looking for a good book to buy. Leave a review on Amazon.com so others can benefit from your wisdom!

With much thanks,

Allie Allen

Printed in Great Britain
by Amazon

36408884R10029